TRANSFORMING YOUR FAITH IN 30 DAYS

RAY PATRICK

COPYRIGHT © 2025 RAY PATRICK. ALL RIGHTS RESERVED.

PUBLISHED BY RAY PATRICK

978-1-326-68018-3

IMPRINT: LULU.COM

This Journal Belongs To

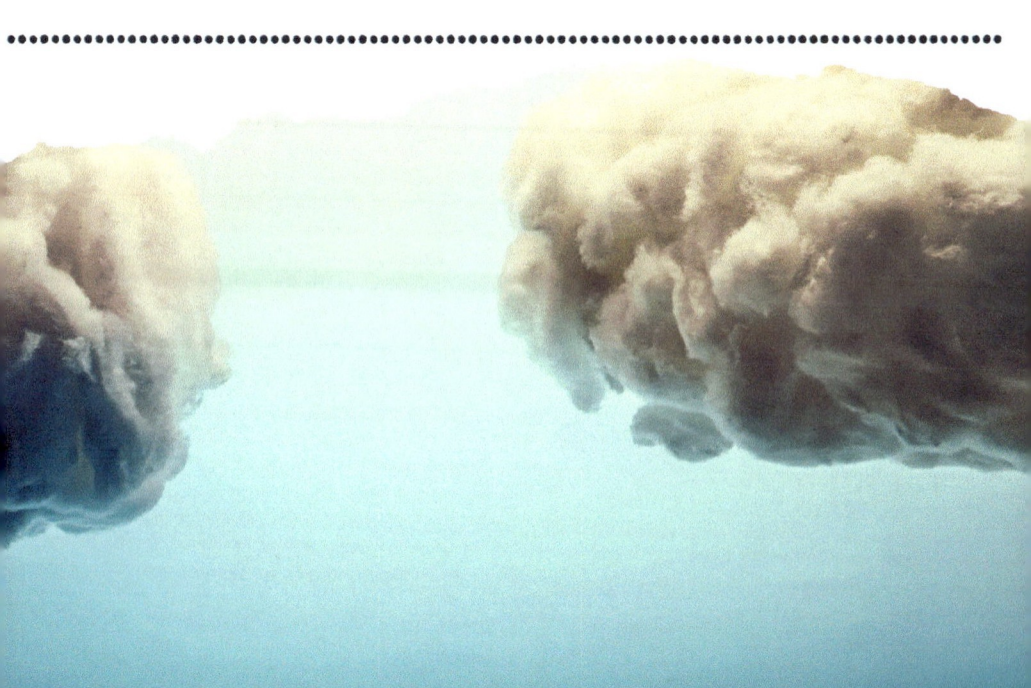

....

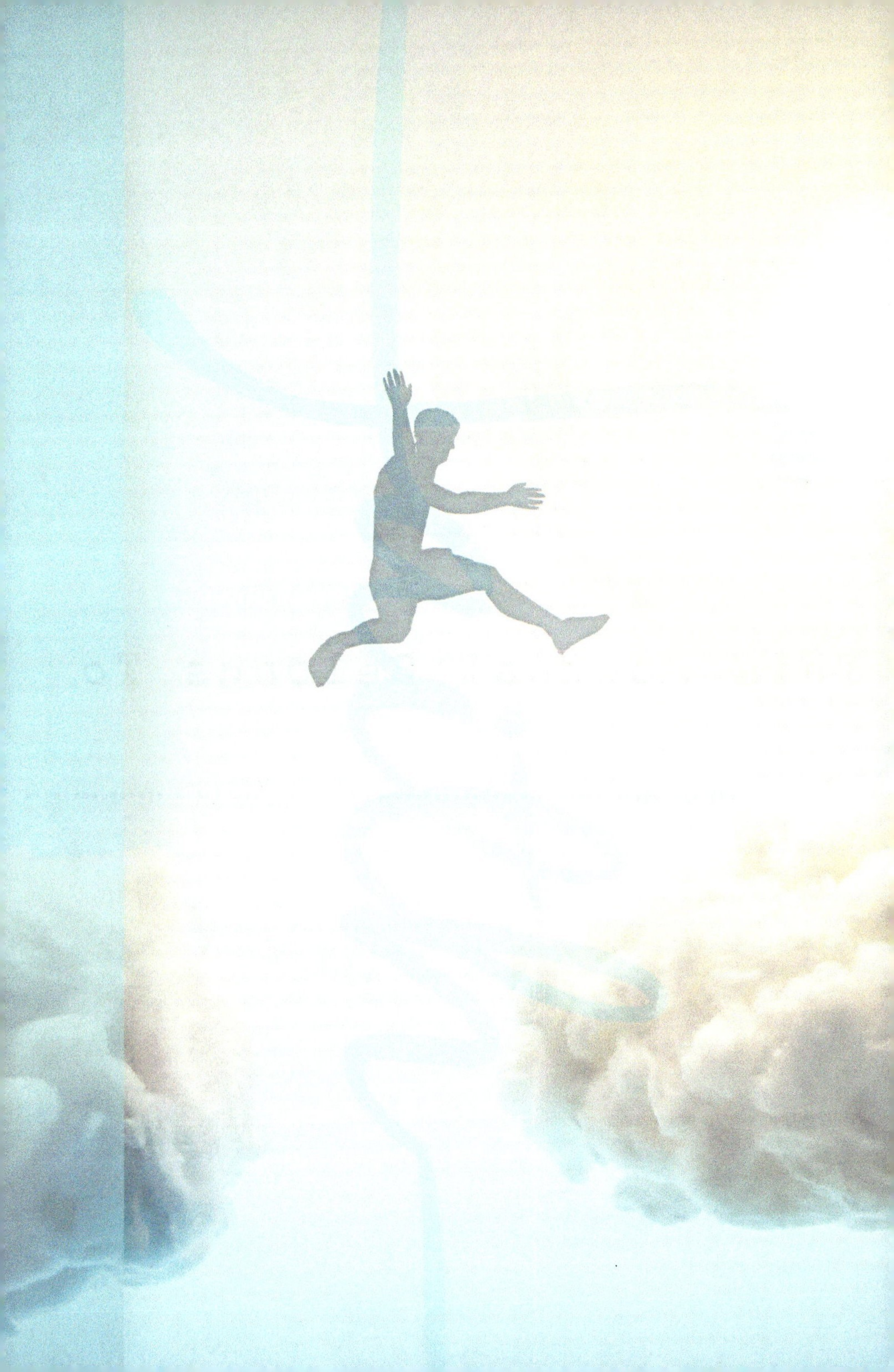

– PREFACE –

Faith that shows the very presence of God is transforming faith. It is moving, alive, and active. In Luke 17, Jesus' disciples boldly ask their teacher to "increase our faith." Jesus explains that even a small amount of faith can do great wonders. Everyone has some faith; everyone trusts something or someone. The object of the Christian faith is what makes all the difference, since Christianity is faith based founded on God, Father, Son, and the Holy Ghost, that is where we place our faith that's where we find transforming faith.

Most people think that faith is "belief without proof," I reject this definition and you should too. Faith is NOT belief despite evidence, but rather it is an all-embracing trust in someone, or something based upon knowledge. This is the very heart of Christianity. To know God is to trust Him and believe Him, and if we don't know Him, the more apt we are to believe in earthly wisdom with its naturalism, materialism, scepticism, and atheism and walk by sight and our own perception. These perceptions are what make us struggle with faith. This is because we don't really know God.

The key to having a transforming faith is to spend more time in God's word getting to know Him. This will remind us of what He has done for us dying on the cross to take away our sins and giving us total forgiveness. Paul in Romans 10:17 states "So then faith cometh by hearing and hearing by the word of God." Faith is in the present. It is not a one-time activity but is continual, so you have to stay in the Word of God.

Matthew 6:33 says faith is seeking God's will and His Kingdom. It is choosing to trust Jesus and not ourselves. Proverbs 3:5 reminds us to: "Trust in the LORD with all thine heart; and lean not unto thine own understanding." And, it is being confident in what we hope and sure of what we do not see. Hebrews 11 puts it this way: "Now faith is the substance of things hoped for, the evidence of things not seen."

⚠ WARNING

FAITH WILL NOT ONLY AFFECT OUR WORDS AND ACTIONS BUT IT WILL ALSO FILTER INTO OUR ATTITUDES AND THOUGHTS...

We will start to think of God's Word and anticipate victory over defeat. Second Corinthians 10:5 describes it as: "Casting down imaginations, and every high thing that exalteth itself against God and bringing into captivity every thought to the obedience of Christ." Transforming faith will cause us to start acting like God acts and to see our victory in advance. When we believe we are on God's team and we are going to win, we begin to understand who we are, and it gives us peace and joy in the Spirit. Worship is the ultimate expression of faith and praise is it's language.

As you read these words be mindful of the disciple Thomas. Thomas hears about the resurrection, but he, as a sceptic, refuses to believe without direct personal experience. Jesus did accommodate Thomas' lack of faith by personally coming to Thomas and allowing him to even touch Him. At this, Thomas reacts in worship and Jesus tells him, "Because you have seen me, you have believed; blessed are those who have not seen and yet have believed." John 20:29. Let me remind you "But without faith it is impossible to please him: for he that cometh to God must believe that he is, and that he is a rewarder of them that diligently seek him." After reading this little book hope you will remember this one thought. Transforming faith is believing in the Word of God and acting upon it instead of responding to human perceptions.

-CONTENTS-

DAY 1	A New Creation
DAY 2	Spiritual Hunger
DAY 3	More Questions Than Answers
DAY 4	Blockage
DAY 5	Be Like The Bumblebee
DAY 6	His Goodness
DAY 7	I've Never Seen Anything Like This Before
DAY 8	Obey God's Word
DAY 9	Our Ancestor In Faith
DAY 10	Ridiculous Laughter
DAY 11	Look Beyond Friday's Problem
DAY 12	Hardship
DAY 13	Don't Worry
DAY 14	The Currency Of Faith
DAY 15	Remember God's Promises
DAY 16	Just Like Hannah
DAY 17	Keep Walking Through
DAY 18	Suffering
DAY 19	Your Faith On Trial
DAY 20	The Music Is Over - Now The Singing Starts
DAY 21	We Just Have To Trust God
DAY 22	Explosive Blessings
DAY 23	God Is Our Refuge
DAY 24	Procrastination
DAY 25	Release What You Cannot Control
DAY 26	It's Time To Retrain Your Mind
DAY 27	Faith That Moves Mountains
DAY 28	Declare It
DAY 29	Be Delivered!
DAY 30	You Will Win!

DAY 1
A NEW CREATION

> Therefore, if anyone is in Christ, he is a new creation; the old has gone, the new has come! (2 Corinthians 5:17)

As a born again child of God, you are a new creation. You have a new spirit and a new life! There may be "old" things in your life that you are trying to get rid of. Maybe you have old habits or addictions that you need to change.

Remember today, that the new has come. It's a new season with fresh opportunities, and it's time for you to be the new, fresh you. Let this be the moment, the day, the year that you break old habits, addictions and old ways of thinking. Let this be the time that you move forward into a new life of victory. So take hold of your spiritual blessings that the Lord has promised — peace, health, protection and victory. Don't let anything pass you by.

Today, be encouraged, because no matter what is happening in your life right now, you have a chance for a new beginning. Choose to leave the old behind — leave behind old behaviours, old words, old mindsets and embrace the new by faith. Trust that He is leading you in this season. Declare His Word and embrace the blessings and victories He has prepared for you!

- A PRAYER OF FAITH -

Yahweh, thank You for making me new. I leave behind the old life and ask that You empower me by Your spirit. Father, help me to understand Your plans for my life, and to embrace the truth of Your Word that sets me free. God, please break my addictions and bad habits. Make me new and whole. Grant me Your peace, health and protection, as I move forward in Christ's name! Amen.

Dear God...

DAY 2
SPIRITUAL HUNGER

> "Blessed are those who hunger and thirst for righteousness, for they will be filled.
> (Matthew 5:6)"

During the lockdown, many were lonely, depressed and going hungry in the natural. What do you do when you're hungry and just not sure when or what will satisfy you? You may try to think of what to eat, but maybe you're not sure when you will get it. Spiritual hunger works the same way. You may feel restless or unsettled, but you can't quite figure out what will satisfy you. You may try to fill that need with other things— addictions, people, or negative behaviour, but only God can fill that spiritual void, and also supply your physical and emotional needs. Reach out to Him today.

In today's verse, we are told what will fill the hunger in our souls – God's righteousness. When you hunger and thirst for righteousness, which is God's way of doing good things, you will be spiritually satisfied. But just like you must take time to eat in the natural, you must take time to "eat" or partake of God's righteousness. Doing right and feasting on His Word.

Today and every day, take time and devote it to the Lord with prayer. State your physical needs, spend time in worship and the study of His Word. Stay in fellowship with other believers by attending church regularly, staying amongst the righteous and doing righteous acts. As you focus your hunger on God's righteousness, you will be filled and live satisfied in Him all the days of your life.

- A PRAYER OF FAITH -

Yahweh, thank You for the promise to fill my hunger both physically and spiritually. Father, I open my heart to You and ask that You draw me by Your Spirit. God, I beg You to teach me to walk in Your ways of righteousness, Your right doing, that I may honour You and be satisfied, physically, emotionally, and spiritually all the days of my life. I receive this by faith right now. I bless You always, in Christ's Name! Amen.

Dear God...

DAY 3
MORE QUESTIONS THAN ANSWERS

> God knows the way that I take; when He has tested me, I will come forth as gold.
> (Job 23:10)

Throughout life, we may experience sorrows for which there are no adequate explanations. Some are difficult events with far-reaching effects, while others are personal, private tragedies that alter our individual lives and families forever. We want to know why, but we seem to find more questions than answers. Yet even as we struggle with "why?" God extends His unfailing love to us.

Some years ago, an experimental spacecraft broke apart during a test flight. The co-pilot died while the pilot miraculously survived. Investigators determined what happened, but not why. The title of a newspaper article about the crash began with the words "Questions remain."

In the bible, Job lost his children and his wealth in a single day. He sank into an angry depression and resisted any attempted explanations by his friends, even though he still had questions. He held out hope that someday there would be an answer from his God. Even with no answers, Job could say, "God knows the way that I take; when He has tested me, I will come forth as gold".

Today, as we face life's unanswered questions, we can find help in God's love and promises that one day, every tear and perplexity, every oppression and distress, every suffering and pain, wrong, and injustice, will have a complete, and powerful explanation. Until then, hold on by faith that the answer is on the way.

- A PRAYER OF FAITH -

Yahweh, thank You for giving me faith and trust in You. So that even though I have questions about life, and why things have happened the way they have, my love for You hasn't wavered. Father, there is one thing I can't and won't question and that is Your love for me. God, give me wisdom and understanding today to accept what I can't explain, believing You know what's best for me. In Christ's name! Amen.

Dear God...

DAY 4
BLOCKAGE

> I will go before you and make the crooked places straight...
> (Isaiah 45:2)

Have you ever felt like every time you try to move forward in something, you hit a blockage, or something happens that throws you off course? Be encouraged today because God has gone before you! You may not see it, but He is preparing a way for you. He's making your crooked places straight. He's making your rough places smooth. You may be going through a difficult time right now, but it's not the end. God has a detour around the blockage, and He has equipped you for this journey!

Remember, don't focus on your circumstances, focus on the promises of God! Keep speaking words of faith because God promises to anoint your head with oil. He'll cause your cup to run over. That means when you seek Him, He will refresh and anoint you to do what He's called you to do.

Today, keep moving forward. Despite the blockage, God can make a way out of no way. Start by checking your attitude. Don't go around complaining and focusing on the negative side of things. Instead, put on an attitude of praise and thanksgiving. Thank Him for removing that blockage and for making your crooked places straight. Keep your eyes on Him and let Him lead you into victory all the days of your life!

- A PRAYER OF FAITH -

Yahweh, thank You for Your goodness in my life. Father, thank You for preparing my path and for making my crooked places straight. God, I give You total permission to remove all the blockages in my life that are stopping me from moving forward. Restore my soul and lead me in the plan You have for me, in Christ's Name! Amen.

Dear God...

DAY 5
BE LIKE THE BUMBLEBEE

> But God hath chosen the foolish things of the world to confound the wise; and God hath chosen the weak things of the world to confound the things which are mighty.
> (1 Corinthians 1:27)

I don't like Bumblebees. I want to get rid of them as soon as I see them. But did you know, that according to all the laws of aerodynamics, a bumblebee should not be able to fly? Its wingspan is too small for the size of its body, it shouldn't get enough lift. But here's the key: nobody told the bumblebee. It didn't get the email. No experts were able to talk it out of flying. The bumblebee felt its wings on its sides and something in its brain said, "I'm supposed to fly, I'm not made to just crawl around".

Have you ever had the experts tell you, "You'll never get well; you'll never get out of debt; this is as good as it gets"? With all due respect, experts can be wrong at times. The experts told Mrs. Patrick that she would never have children. Yet today she has 4 children, 18 grandchildren and 10 great grand children. The experts told me that because of my past sins and addictions, I will never be a successful minister. Praise God! I'm doing pretty good in Jesus name! Each day through my devotional blog, school, radio and other ministries, over 10,000 people are being blessed.

Today, there will be times you have to believe God over the experts and even human logic. Watch what He will do on your behalf! You will be able to fly, have a good job, be educated, own your home, have children and develop ministries that will bless others. Don't settle for less than God has in store for you.

- A PRAYER OF FAITH -

Yahweh, thank You for Your goodness and faithfulness in my life. Today, I cast aside logic and apply faith in You. I believe You over what the "experts" tell me and what humans want me to believe. I believe that You are faithful and expect to see Your goodness all the days of my life. In Jesus' name, Amen.

Dear God...

DAY 6
HIS GOODNESS

> I remain confident of this: I will see the goodness of the Lord in the land of the living.
> (Psalm 27:13)

In these uncertain times, we can learn the attitude of the psalmist David, who was going through very tough uncertain times when he declared the words in today's verse. He said in effect, "I'm not worried. I'm not upset. I am confident I will see God's goodness". In other words, "This situation I'm in may be rough, but that's not going to steal my vision or joy. It's not going to cause me to give up on my dreams. I am confident that in this crazy unpredictable year, I will see God's favour unfold in my life".

Remember, what you focus on is what will come to pass. No matter what the medical report says, no matter what your finances look like, no matter how bad that relationship may seem, be confident that you will see God's goodness unfold in your life!

Today, during these strange times, we must not forget our God is Omnipotent, Omniscient, and Omnibenevolent. He is the creator of the universe, and He holds you, your plans, and your dreams in the palm of His hand. So, you can be confident nothing is too difficult for Him! Take hold of this truth by faith and focus on His goodness today!

- A PRAYER OF FAITH -

Yahweh, thank You for Your goodness in my life. Father, I remain confident in Your power to control my life in these uncertain times. I will focus on You no matter what my circumstances may look like. God, please give me Your peace as I keep my mind stayed on You. In Christ's name, Amen.

Dear God...

DAY 7
I'VE NEVER SEEN ANYTHING LIKE THIS BEFORE

> Being confident of this, that He who began a good work in you will carry it on to completion until the day of Christ Jesus.
> (Philippians 1:6)

Is your breakthrough taking longer than you hoped? Have you been praying for a loved one, or maybe you believed that a situation would change for years? Don't get discouraged. God is going to finish what He started! He is faithful, and He has something unmatched, unparalleled coming your way. Breakthroughs and restoration, like you haven't seen before – Hallelujah!

God has been good to us, but I believe we're coming into a time of greater anointing, greater power, and greater victories! The key is that we must stay in agreement with God. We should get up every morning and say, "Father, thank You for Your unprecedented favour. Thank You for the immeasurable, unlimited, surpassing greatness of Your power". If you keep standing in faith, I believe you're going to come into more of those days where you stand in utter amazement and say, "WOW, God! I've never seen anything like this before!"

Today, remember the question that Scripture asks, "is there anything too hard for the Lord?" and the answer is "no", nothing is impossible when we put our faith and trust in Him. So, keep standing, believing, and hoping, because God has something astounding in store for your future. He will finish what He started!

- A PRAYER OF FAITH -

Yahweh, today I give my heart and my mind to You, so You can finish what You started in me. Father, I trust and believe that You are working on my behalf. God, I will stand strong on Your promises today, knowing that victory is mine, in Christ's Name! Amen.

Dear God...

DAY 8
OBEY GOD'S WORD

> Master, we've worked hard all night ... But because you say so, I will let down the nets.
> (Luke 5:5)

As an evangelist, this story here fascinates me and goes against most views on traditional evangelism. Listening to the experts who have been to seminary, the norm was to fish when fish were ripe and ready - mainly at night or in dark times, and to avoid a crowd as it would chase the fish away. Simon Peter was quite sure he knew more about fishing than Jesus did. But he was about to be pleasantly surprised.

Andrew introduced Peter to Jesus, and Peter had seen how Jesus healed his mother-in-law from a high fever. Yet, he was not fully convinced by Jesus, so he continued fishing.

Scripture says one day Jesus used Simon Peter's boat to speak to the crowd. Later Jesus told Simon to row out into deep water and let down the nets for a catch. Simon likely thought, "That's a dumb thing to do. The night is the best time for fishing". But after explaining that they'd fished all night and caught nothing, he muttered, "Because if you say so ..." and obeyed. What an awesome result! They caught so many fish that the nets began to break.

Today we can learn important lessons from Simon Peter's encounter with Christ in Luke 5. Fishing/ evangelism is all about faith in Jesus. Reverence before him, dependence on his wisdom and power, and obedience to his Word. His doubts about Christ were gone. The evidence was in the nets. Jesus had such amazing power, that he had to be the Son of God! Peter's sense of unworthiness in Jesus' presence brought him to his knees.

- A PRAYER OF FAITH -

Yahweh, forgive my weak faith, superficial worship, and shoddy obedience. Father, deepen my awareness of your greatness and my dependence on you. God help me to look beyond my own self-reliance and become more reliant on you. In Jesus' name, Amen.

Dear God...

DAY 9
OUR ANCESTOR IN FAITH

> The Lord your God is God in heaven above and on the earth below.
> (Joshua 2:11)

The harlot, Rahab, took a great risk in hiding the Israelite spies. She did that because she recognized the Israelites could not have crossed the Red Sea or survived forty years in the wilderness on their own power. She saw that God was the source of their strength. Though she was an outsider from Jericho, she understood who God is and what God can do.

Through the grace and mercy of God, this woman who was a prostitute and an outsider, served as a witness to truth and a role model of faith. God used her story to remind Israel that they were not chosen because they were a great and mighty nation; they were chosen to be God's people because of God's compassion and mercy. God also chose Rahab.

We read Rahab became an ancestor of David. Matthew lists her in Jesus' family tree, and the Book of James names her as an example of Christian hospitality. The book of Hebrews also includes her in the roll call of heroes of faith. Rahab is our ancestor in faith. She saw that God was doing something new in the world, and God made her a part of it.

Today, we also know that God is doing something new in the world by faith. God is sending his Son to establish His Kingdom. We look forward with faith, expectation, and hope to his return to reign forever. Come, Lord Jesus!

- A PRAYER OF FAITH -

Yahweh, "God in heaven above and on the earth below", we bow in worship before you. Father build our faith like Rahab's, so that we will have hope of your coming kingdom which will bring us deliverance. In Jesus' name, Amen.

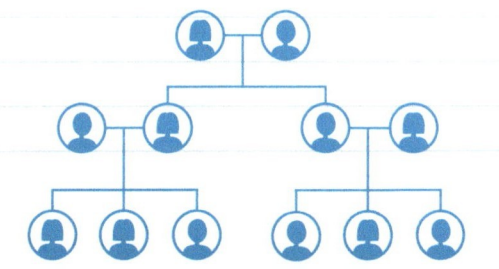

Dear God...

DAY 10
RIDICULOUS LAUGHTER

> Sarah said, "God has brought me laughter, and everyone who hears about this will laugh with me. (Genesis 21:6)

Has God ever surprised you with the ridiculous? Has He promised you something that seems impossible? Have you ever thought that God is taking too long because there is no time left? You're not alone. Sarah was ninety years old when she became the mother of Isaac. When the Lord visited Abraham a year earlier and told him they would have a son, she laughed. Sarah thought it was impossible — and perhaps even ridiculous.

Shortly after that, she held her newborn son in her arms, understanding that, God had the last laugh. Now she laughed with Him not because the situation was surprising, funny or ridiculous, but because it was so wondrous. She even named her son child Isaac, which means "laughter".

Today, are you waiting on God for the ridiculous? Is He taking too long? Abraham and Sarah's long years of disappointment at not having a child and waiting on God to keep His promise ended in the joy of welcoming their beautiful baby boy. God had indeed brought laughter and hope, the beginning of the fulfilment of His promise to make them parents of a great nation. His faithfulness to them is one example of how God is faithful to us. God wants to birth laughter and joy in you right now, to end sin, suffering and death.

- A PRAYER OF FAITH -

Yahweh, thank you for your promises. Father, please give me patients as I await answers and hold on to the ridiculous and the miraculous. Just like Sarah and Abraham, keep me laughing until my breakthrough comes. Today I celebrate the birth of joy and no more sin, suffering, Sorrow and death in Jesus' name. Amen.

Dear God...

DAY 11
LOOK BEYOND FRIDAY'S PROBLEMS

> Always be joyful. Never stop praying. Be thankful in all circumstances, for this is God's will for you who belong to Christ Jesus.
> (1 Thessalonians 5:16-18)

On Easter weekend, where the focus is on the death, burial and resurrection of Christ, joy - not sorrow - should be our spiritual response. Did you know that it's God's will for you to be joyful always? God wants you to be happy and carefree. He wants you to love your life no matter what your circumstances look like. When you have joy during difficult circumstances, it's evidence that you have faith and trust that God is going to bring you through.

In Christ, joy is strength. When you have His joy, you can stand strong, no matter who or what wants to crucify you. You might say, "I'm just not a real jovial person. I'm more serious. I never laugh much". I do realise God made us all differently, but you still can experience real inward joy, which should externally make you happy and excited. So let yourself laugh and have fun because that's why Christ came, died then rose. I read where the average child laughs over 200 times a day, but the average adult only laughs 4 times a day. What happened? We've allowed the pressures of life, stress, and responsibilities to steal our joy.

Today, decide to get your joy back. Decide that you are going to look beyond Friday's problems, and towards Sunday's resurrection and hope. Know that God will see you through. Ask Him every day to fill you with His supernatural peace and joy, so that you can live in Christ's strength and victory all the days of your life!

- A PRAYER OF FAITH -

Yahweh, I humbly receive Your Word today. Father, I choose to open my heart to You and invite You to fill me with Your joy and strength that the resurrection brings. Yahshua, thank You for showing me Your goodness and empowering me with Your grace. I bless You today for Your amazing sacrifice, in Christ's Name! Amen.

Dear God...

DAY 12
HARDSHIP

> Let us run with perseverance the race marked out for us, fixing our eyes on Jesus, the pioneer and perfecter of faith. For the joy set before Him He endured the cross, scorning its shame, and sat down at the right hand of the throne of God.
> (Hebrews 12:1-2)

Experiencing hardship is never easy. In fact, it can be agonizing, exhausting, and depressing. There have been times in my life when I have instantly sensed God's awesome presence with me during a difficult circumstance. But there have been even more instances when it seemed as though God was nowhere to be found.

While Jesus was in the garden of Gethsemane awaiting His fate, His sweat was like drops of blood falling to the ground as He prayed. He knew that what He was about to endure was going to be excruciatingly difficult. He didn't even hesitate to ask God if He could be spared from the suffering. Jesus felt utterly alone. Even His friends had fallen asleep during the most crucial moment in his life.

Not only did Jesus ask if His cup of suffering could pass, but He prayed for strength and embraced the will of His heavenly Father who gave Him the power to endure.

Today, no one enjoys going through trials, especially alone. But in these moments, God asks us to trust Him. Hard times will pass. But with patience, prayer, and a heart full of hope and trust, we can live through them – knowing God can give us lasting peace and deep joy that will outlast any pain and sorrow.

- A PRAYER OF FAITH -

Yahweh, thank You, for the gift of Your Holy Spirit which comforts me during the difficult times in my life. Father, I ask for Your strength to empower me, and for hope to fill my heart. God, I walk through this current situation trusting You and believing that You have something good in store for me and those around me. Lord, I open my heart to Your will and Your way. In Jesus' name, Amen.

Dear God...

DAY 13
DON'T WORRY

> Can any one of you by worrying add a single hour to your life?
> (Matthew 6:27)

With casualties going up in wars around the globe, and the economy the weakest it's ever been, it's easy to worry. What are you worrying about today? To worry means to allow something to revolve in your mind repeatedly until it stresses you out. God doesn't want you to live worried or anxious about anything. He knows that worry steals your peace and joy. It affects every area of your life negatively. Have you heard the saying, "Don't worry yourself sick"? That's because worrying affects your physical and mental body. It even affects your sleep.

The Bible says you won't ever gain anything by worrying; in fact, you'll lose precious moments that you can never get back again. The good news is that God has promised that you can have victory over worry. It starts by choosing to trust in Him. When you cast your cares on Him, He will give you His peace, which will eradicate your worry. Hallelujah!

Today, why not put an end to worry in your life. Choose to feed your faith and fill your mind with God's promises of peace. As you focus on God's Word and spend time in conversation with Him, He will drive out worry and fill your heart with faith and expectancy, and you will overcome in every area of your life!

- A PRAYER OF FAITH -

Yahweh, today I permit You to put an end to worry in my life. Father, I have decided to feed my faith by studying Your promises and declaring Your Word over my life. God, help me to trust in You today and every day, in Christ's Name! Amen.

Dear God...

DAY 14
THE CURRENCY OF FAITH

> And whatever you ask for in prayer, having faith and [really] believing, you will receive. (Matthew 21:22)

Everyone needs money – it is the currency of our world. In the natural, we exchange money for the things we want and need. But in the supernatural or spiritual realm, faith is our currency and what we exchange for what we need or want.

The Bible tells us that when we pray if we have faith, we will receive what we pray for.
Faith is heaven's currency. Faith moves mountains. Faith opens doors. Faith pleases God. What is faith you may ask? It is simply believing and trusting God and His Word. It's believing in His goodness and knowing that He is a rewarder of those who diligently seek after Him. Faith is trusting that the promises of God are true. It's obeying His Word. Where does faith come from? Everyone is given a measure of faith. Romans tells us that faith grows by hearing the Word of God.

Today, the more you hear the Word of God, the more real it becomes in your life, and the easier it is to believe His promises. It doesn't matter how much faith you have today, begin investing your faith in God's Word so that your trust will grow. As you hear and obey the Word, you will be empowered to move forward to receive every good gift God has in store for you.

- A PRAYER OF FAITH -

Yahweh, thank You for the supernatural currency of faith which gives Your Word power to work in my life. Father, I submit myself to You today and ask that the seeds of faith in my heart grow stronger with each new day. God, I trust You and I open my heart to You and ask You to remove doubt and unbelief, so that I can trust and serve You with my whole heart, all in Christ's Name! Amen.

Dear God...

DAY 15
REMEMBER GOD'S PROMISES

> "Keep this Book of the Law always on your lips; meditate on it day and night, so that you may be careful to do everything written in it. Then you will be prosperous and successful.
> (Joshua 1:8)

Within the past year, many things may not have gone the way anyone expected. When things don't go the way you planned, or something unexpected happens, how do you respond? Do you start expecting the worst, or do you go to God's Word and remind yourself of His promises?

Faith comes by hearing the Word of God. Faith activates God's promises. When difficulties come and you're tempted to get upset, remind yourself of His Word and declare, "this is not going to prosper against me. They may be talking about me. It may look bad, but I know God is my vindicator. He'll take care of me. I know God has me in the palm of His hands."

Today, remind yourself of God's promises. You don't have to get worried. You know God is still on the throne. You know that problem didn't come to stay; it came to pass. So today, remind yourself of His promises and feed your faith, so that you can move forward in the life of blessing He has prepared for you!

- A PRAYER OF FAITH -

Yahweh, thank You for every one of Your amazing promises. Father, I choose to meditate on Your Word which brings life to me. Almighty God, fill me with Your peace as I stand in faith, until I see the victory You have promised me come to pass in my life, in Jesus' Name! Amen.

Dear God...

DAY 16
JUST LIKE HANNAH

> *I am a woman who is deeply troubled. . . . I was pouring out my soul to the Lord.*
> (1 Samuel 1:15)

In the Old Testament, Hannah desperately wanted children. Every year, when her family went to worship at Shiloh, she judged herself to be a failure by her culture's standards. One day it broke her. She was in deep anguish; she couldn't eat, and all she could do was weep. No one could comfort her. Despite the hopelessness of her situation, Hannah prayed and turned to the Holy One, who "had closed her womb."

With all of her emotions, she begged God to attend to her helplessness and grant her a son. In her prayer, Hannah trusted that God heard her and cared about her and would answer her cry. God did hear Hallelujah! God gave Hannah the gift of a son.

Today, when we experience dark days and seasons of grief and despair, like Hannah in the bible, we can cry out to God and claim His faithfulness. In such moments we are called to remember the story and love of our generous, gracious God—the God of hope, the God who will make right what is wrong in our lives, the God who will overturn all that causes us grief. Just like Hannah's prayer was answered with a son, our moments of desperation, despair and discouragement can be reversed with the gift of God's son Jesus Christ. Why not try Him today.

- A PRAYER OF FAITH -

Yahweh, thank you that when I'm in darkness and I cry out to you, you always come through. God help me to remember that your Son is my light who came to take away my despair and show me the way to abundant life. In your name Christ, we pray. Amen.

Dear God...

DAY 17
KEEP WALKING THROUGH

> Yea, though I walk through the valley of the shadow of death, I will fear no evil; for You are with me...
> (Psalm 23:4)

Do you feel right now that you're walking through the valley of the shadow of death? This refers to life's tough times when you're at breaking point, evil is all around you, and fear steals your faith.

During these tough times, it's easy to get discouraged. I love what it says in the verse, "though I walk through...". So, no matter what evil you are facing today, know this: you are not alone, and you are just walking through. You don't have to stop and live in the tough times, just keep walking through. They are only temporary. Hallelujah!

Today, don't allow fear to paralyse you in the middle of "the valley of the shadow of death". Remember, God is with you. He is walking beside you. He is strengthening you. He is making a way of escape for you. He is lining up people and situations to bring you out of that tough place into a place of strength and victory. Don't give up! Press on and walkthrough, staying focused as you walk. Have a vision of your life on the other side of the valley. See yourself more loving, more faithful, stronger, and more blessed than ever before. As you keep moving forward and walking through, you will get to the other side and experience God's victory!

- A PRAYER OF FAITH -

Yahweh, thank You for Your faithfulness toward me. Father, thank You for walking with me in the hard times of life when I feel like giving up and giving in. God, I won't stay or stop in my negative, discouraging, or evil trial, I will keep walking forward keeping my eyes on You. I trust that You will carry me and care for me as I go through my valley, to a place of victory and strength, in Christ's Name! Amen.

Dear God...

DAY 18
SUFFERING

> "Blessed is the one who perseveres under trial because, having stood the test, that person will receive the crown of life that the Lord has promised to those who love him
> (James 1: 12)"

Suffering is a human reality. Christians are not exempt from the results of suffering. The Apostles suffered greatly and many of them died horrendous deaths. But it was all for God's glory and a part of His divine plan for their lives.

When trials come your way, unexpectedly, do you shake your fist, or do you trust God's ways are higher than yours? Do you say to God, "Not my will, but Yours be done"? Do you trust that He will use that terrible trial for your good and for His glory? God will use all things to make us to the image of His Son and often in the life of the believer that may include pain and suffering. But In times of suffering, He gives us coping mechanisms. Pray for God's mercy to come, cry out for His help and we will one day taste of victory. Hallelujah!

Today, please remember there is a day that awaits every believer, where all pain and suffering will cease. That is why we must keep our eyes fixed upon the hope of eternity and not on this life. And that is why faith in God is so important. It is the rock on which we stand when trials come (and they will). We must remember the hope that God will never leave our side and walks with us through the valley experiences. We also have the ultimate hope of eternal life that awaits us in Christ. That is our anchor during hard times - the hope of eternity.

- A PRAYER OF FAITH -

Yahweh, thank you for being with me in my suffering. Father, please help me find your mercy and goodness when trials come and not grumble and complain. Holy Spirit convict my heart and remind me to be thankful for your promises. God, in my suffering, may I look forward to heaven and the crown of life that awaits me. Today I stand firm in faith, trusting you. So, I won't fear. I love you for not allowing me to be alone in my suffering. In Christ' name, Amen.

Dear God...

DAY 19
YOUR FAITH ON TRIAL

> God said, 'Take your son, your only son, whom you love—Isaac—and... sacrifice him... as a burnt offering'.
> (Genesis 22:2)

Abraham's life is one of the most fascinating in scripture. His journey of faith involved some painful twists and turns. Isaac's story must be the most difficult for every parent. Here, God tests Abraham by telling him to offer up his son, Isaac, as a sacrifice, and Abraham nearly goes through with it!

It's an unthinkable request to ask Abraham to offer up his own son. After all, this was the son of promise. The one through whom God promised to bless the nations of the world. This command likely made no sense to Abraham. Isaac was God's great gift. But now it seemed that this gift was to be given back to God. Could Abraham let go of his son? The one thing that meant more to him than life itself? And what about God's promise to bless the nations through him? It now seemed a long way away.

Today, as I look at the request from God to kill Isaac, it was surely a challenging, excruciating test of Abraham's faith. But he had learned to trust God enough to provide a solution. He even told Isaac, "God himself will provide the lamb for the burnt offering, my son". At times our faith may be tested too. Will we trust God to keep his promises, however challenging it may be to obey? Through Jesus, God's only Son who laid down his life for our sake, we can trust God for a positive outcome.

- A PRAYER OF FAITH -

Yahweh, give me a deep trusting faith in you. Father, help me to know that you will see me through every trial, and you keep your promises. In Jesus's name, Amen.

Dear God...

DAY 20
THE MUSIC IS OVER - NOW THE SINGING STARTS

> The young men have stopped their music. Joy is gone from our hearts...
> (Lamentations 5:14-15)

Right now, we may feel as if nothing will ever again be right in our lives. Some feel beaten down and afraid to have hope. Or perhaps we have heard of a better day, and yet we are filled with despair. The music is over!

In the book of Lamentations, we have many funeral songs for Jerusalem and its people after the city was destroyed. Jeremiah confesses God's sovereignty and justice, but he also can't shake off the feeling of rejection and pain. He cries out, "Why do you forsake us so long?". You may feel like this today, but please know that Jesus understands. He was mocked by his enemies as he hung dying on the cross. He was forsaken by his closest friends. He even cried out, "My God, my God, why have you forsaken me?". But God raised Him from the grave and "gave Him a new name". God hears your cry and is willing to lift you from the pit of despair.

Today be like Jeremiah in scripture who looked beyond his despair to God's promise of deliverance, that's why he could sing with words of faith that have given believers hope through the ages: "Because of the Lord's great love we are not consumed, for his compassions never fail. They are new every morning; great is your faithfulness" (Lamentations 3). Hallelujah!

- A PRAYER OF FAITH -

Yahweh thank you for hearing my cry of despair. Father, today I receive your promise of deliverance, just like Jeremiah. And I sing like him "Great is thy faithfulness, O God my Father. Morning by morning new mercies I see", Hallelujah! Thank you, Lord! Amen.

Dear God...

DAY 21
WE JUST HAVE TO TRUST GOD

> "The Lord gave and the Lord has taken away; may the name of the Lord be praised.
> (Job 1:21)

In the bible, Job was not perfect. After he suffered devastating losses, he shook an angry fist at God and demanded that God explain why. It's no wonder he was angry. His children (all 10 of them!) died when their house collapsed, and all the rest of his possessions were burned by fires or stolen by thieves. Still, Job was an upright man who feared God and shunned evil.

What do good men and women do when faced with great loss? They likely experience a wide range of emotions, but in the end, they look to God; they lean on God; they trust God. They learn to say: "Every blessing you pour out I'll turn to praise. When the darkness closes in, Lord, still I will say, Blessed be the name of the Lord."

Today in the book of Job, God answers Job's plea of "Why?", with a series of questions. Through the swirling puzzles God sets before Job, God gives a non-answer and the best answer as to why so much devastation visited him. God gave Job a 'weak' answer that is the strongest of all: "Job, you can't understand. You'll just have to trust me". So, it is in much of our lives. We just have to trust God because we won't understand.

- A PRAYER OF FAITH -

Yahweh, teach me to leave my burning unanswered questions with you and simply trust you. Father, Your ways are not my ways, so give me the faith to believe that you know best. Today Lord, I trust you with my unexplained "whys" and like Job 'blessed be the name of the Lord". In Jesus's name, Amen.

Dear God...

DAY 22
EXPLOSIVE BLESSINGS

> ...I am making a way in the desert and streams in the wasteland.
> (Isaiah 43:19)

Sometimes I think we are too quick to give up. Or we look at God in the natural and not the supernatural. So often, people limit themselves in their thinking. They don't think they'll ever accomplish their dreams. They start thinking they don't have the talent, the connections or the funds. They don't think a marriage could ever be restored or they'll ever get out of debt. But that kind of thinking comes from looking at your God through natural eyes.

We have to remember that God is a supernatural. And just because we don't see a way, does not mean that God doesn't have a way. God can bring one opportunity across your path that will thrust you to a new level. He has explosive blessings that can blast you out of debt and into abundance! He can do what medical science can't do! Hallelujah!

Today, I encourage you to take the limits off your thinking. Lift up your eyes to Jesus, the Author and Finisher of your faith. Trust that He is working on your behalf, and He will make a way out of no way. Remember, what you are facing may seem impossible with man, but when God puts His "super" on your "natural", anything is possible!

- A PRAYER OF FAITH -

Yahweh, thank You for Your explosive blessings in my life. I invite you to help me see things in the supernatural, as appose to the natural. Help me to take the limits off my thoughts and faith so I can see with a new supernatural perspective. Father, today I choose to lift up my eyes to You. In Jesus name, the Author and Finisher of my faith, Amen!

Dear God...

DAY 23
GOD IS OUR REFUGE

> God is our refuge and strength, an ever-present help in trouble.
> (Psalm 46:1)

The first words of today's Psalm, announces its overall theme: God is our refuge-our fortress and shelter. God is also our strength, our help-the one who deals with the perils surrounding us. And because God is our refuge and help, we have nothing to fear, even if nature throws its worst tantrums at us.

True faith is always tested by the storms and earthquakes in one's life. Where can I find safety and security you may ask? Psalm 46 gives us the answer: "God is our refuge and strength, an ever-present help in trouble. Therefore, we will not fear, though the earth give way. . .."

Today ask yourself the question, 'in what ways has God been my refuge and strength?'. There is a certain and trustworthy basis for our faith-the God who made us and everything in our world. In all circumstances, no matter how terrible or frightening, our unchanging God is our refuge and strength.

- A PRAYER OF FAITH -

Yahweh, thank you for being my refuge and strength. Father, please help me to remember this when my world shakes and my heart trembles with fear. Today oh God, shelter me in your strong, safe arms. In Christ's name, Amen.

Dear God...

DAY 24
PROCRASTINATION

> For the turning away of the simple will slay them, and the complacency of fools will destroy them. (Proverbs 1:32)

Last night, I was talking about spiritual procrastination, and the danger of not taking God-given opportunities, and not using our spiritual gifts. God will never ask you to do something without giving you the ability to do it. You may get passive or complacent and think, "yes, I know I need to do that. Maybe next week"... Well, before you know it, next week turns into next month. Next month turns into next year and so on.

Remember, when we put off what God has told us to do, we miss that season of grace. But if you'll deal with things as soon as God brings them to light, you'll have a special grace, a special empowerment. You'll feel God's enabling power helping you to do it, and you will avoid many trials and pitfalls.

Today, is there something you're putting off? Something you know in your heart that you are supposed to do? Don't let the season pass. Don't let complacency destroy you. Your destiny stands before you. God has something amazing for your future. Be bold; be strong. Step out in faith, be obedient, and embrace the good things God has in store for you!

- A PRAYER OF FAITH -

Yahweh, thank You for the grace to do and enjoy exactly what You've called me to do. Father, I will step out in faith and not procrastinate and miss out on my God-given opportunity. God, I will follow Your commands. Help me to be faithful like You are faithful. I love You and bless You today and always, in Christ's Name! Amen.

Dear God...

DAY 25
RELEASE WHAT YOU CANNOT CONTROL

> Cast your burden on the Lord, and he will sustain you; he will never permit the righteous to be moved.
> (Psalm 55:22)

So often in life, we hold on too tightly to things we were never meant to control. It's hard sometimes, to let go. Struggling to change things and striving hard to maintain order, but when problems mount high and pressures feel overwhelming, we begin to understand more fully how little control we have.

We look in all different places for help, forgetting we can move to our Saviour. We forget that He never changes, and He still holds the power to heal and set free. At times we don't believe that He can, or wants to work on our behalf. We forget that He's still the God of miracles, that He can act "immediately", that He can do in a moment what might take years for us to work out on our own.

Today set aside your fears and move towards the saviour, with faith. Move-in close, and reach out to the One who is All-powerful, compassionate, loving, and kind. He knows the wounds and troubles you carry; He knows the pain and worries you feel. He knows how much you try to let go, and fix things. Please trust that your situation or circumstance is not too big for His healing and freedom. God is Able. He is always within reach. He is never far away. He is close. He is with us. He cares. He heals. He restores. He redeems.

- A PRAYER OF FAITH -

Yahweh, I confess my need for you today. I need your healing and your grace. Father, forgive me for trying to fix my situation by myself forgetting how much I need you, above everyone and everything else. I come to you and bring my hurt. God, You see where no one else fully can. You know the pain I carry. The burdens. The cares. You know where I need to be set free. Cover every broken place. Every wound. Every heartache. Thank you that you can do far more than I could ever imagine. In Christ's name, Amen.

Dear God...

LET IT GO

DAY 26
IT'S TIME TO RETRAIN YOUR MIND

> Do not be conformed to this world (this age), [fashioned after and adapted to its external, superficial customs], but be transformed (changed) by the [entire] renewal of your mind...
> (Romans 12:2)

Repeatedly I hear people say, "I just want to be happy". Many people today don't realize that the reason they're not happy, the reason they're not enjoying life, is simply that they've trained their minds in the wrong direction. They've trained their minds to worry. They've trained their minds to complain. They've trained their minds to see the negative. But, just as you can form these negative mindsets, you can retrain your mind according to the Word of God and form Godly mindsets.

One of the keys to retraining your mind and developing a positive attitude is by learning to stay grateful. When you stay grateful, you are focusing on what's right rather than what's wrong. The seed of the Word takes root in the good ground of your heart. This doesn't happen automatically; you must discipline yourself. You must make a conscious effort every single day, until a good habit is formed.

Today remember, when you live with an attitude of praise and thanksgiving, you are shielding yourself from the attacks of the enemy. The seeds of discouragement cannot take root in a grateful heart. Neither can bitterness, envy, or strife. So, retrain your mind and be empowered with His strength to overcome in every area of your life!

- A PRAYER OF FAITH -

Yahweh, I surrender my thoughts and mind to You. Father, help me retrain my thoughts so that they are in line with Your Word and Your will. God, show me how to have lasting happiness no matter how things turn out. I claim joy over sadness and contentment over confusion. I choose to have an attitude of faith and expectancy. Thank You for empowering me to live the life You have for me. In Christ's name, Amen.

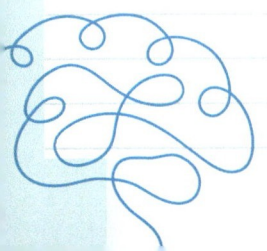

Dear God...

DAY 27
FAITH THAT MOVES MOUNTAINS

> When Jesus saw their faith, he said, 'Friend, your sins are forgiven'.
> (Luke 5:20)

Perhaps you have heard the phrase "Faith can move mountains". I've always marvelled at that phrase. I've seen many mountains. I've visited Kilimanjaro in Africa and lived near the Rockies, and the Sierra Nevada, in the western United States. The mountains are huge. They are ancient geological barriers that can weather any storm. They are solid, enduring, strong, and unyielding.

Scripture says faith in Jesus is even stronger and bigger. The faith of the friends in today's verse, is strong enough to tear apart a roof to bring their paralyzed friend to Jesus – because they had confidence he could heal their friend. Jesus is so moved by their faith that he does what they want him to do and he doesn't even criticize them for damaging the roof! Because people are more important than buildings. The amazing thing is that Jesus does even more than they hoped. He forgives the man's sins as well as healing him from paralysis. In this way, the friends' faith become an example to everyone there who has come to see Jesus.

Today, faith can move people to do incredible things. In response, Jesus can make huge impacts in this world, including moving mountains in our lives. He can heal and forgive. He can change the heart of an individual or the hearts of an entire group of people (which could be more difficult than moving a mountain). This is all because of Christ's ability to see faith in anyone who comes to him, whether they walk or are carried by their friends.

- A PRAYER OF FAITH -

Yahweh, thank you for the gift of faith. Father, please build faith inside of me so I can see how you call me to act, trusting me to make changes for good in this world. God may I never doubt your ability to move the mountains in my life. In Jesus's name, Amen.

Dear God...

DAY 28
DECLARE IT

> Let the redeemed of the Lord say so, whom He has delivered from the hand of the adversary.
> (Psalm 107:2)

"Let the redeemed of the Lord say so". That's what today's Scripture begins with. It doesn't say, "let the redeemed of the Lord think so" or, "let the redeemed believe so". Of course, it's important to think right and believe right, but something supernatural happens when we open our mouths and declare something so emphatically that You don't even have to say it to anyone else.

You can say it while driving or in the shower. Say, "The economy may be low, but I am blessed. I am prosperous. I will lend and not borrow. I may have had some setbacks, but I know those setbacks are a setup for a comeback! This is still going to be my best year so far. The favour of God is turning things around"! You are prophesying positively into your future.

Today, remember when you say what the Lord has done for you, you are declaring that you are redeemed, you are opening the door for God to move on your behalf. The Scripture tells us that He watches over His Word to perform it. When you declare His Word, when you speak His promises, He is faithful to fulfil them, and lead you into victory all the days of your life!

- A PRAYER OF FAITH -

Yahweh, thank You for delivering me and setting me free. Father, I will declare Your goodness. I will declare Your promises. I will declare Your favour, because You told me in Your Word let the redeemed of the Lord say so or declare it so. Hallelujah! God, I know what I declare with my mouth will allow me to live the good life You have prepared for me, in Christ's Name! Amen.

Dear God...

DAY 29
BE DELIVERED!

> Many are the afflictions of the righteous, but the LORD delivers him out of them all.
> (Psalm 34:19)

It's one thing to be forgiven of sin, however, there is still a need for deliverance. God is a mighty Deliverer! You may feel afflicted, overwhelmed, or burdened by the cares of life. God is working to bring you out of that difficult situation. It may not be in the way you thought, but you must trust that God has your best interests at heart.

Consequences and afflictions can take on different forms. Sickness, hardship, temptation, a difficult co-worker, a friend or maybe a contentious family member. There are so many things that can come against us. Remember, those afflictions are only temporary. Stand in faith today believing that God is on your side. It doesn't matter what your circumstances look like, why don't you get up every morning and say, "this is the day that the Lord has made; I will rejoice and be glad in it"!

Today, because of life's afflictions and hardships, you may not feel like rejoicing or being upbeat, but look to God with eyes of faithful expectancy – you'll see your Deliverer is coming. Hallelujah! As you stand and trust the Lord, He will deliver you and empower you to overcome all evil afflictions, and you'll see His abundant blessings in every area of your life.

- A PRAYER OF FAITH -

Yahweh, thank You for being my Deliverer! Father, thanks for the promise to deliver me from all evil and afflictions. I trust that You have a plan for me to not only be sinless but to be spiritually cleansed from my evil ways. God, I thank You for Your strength and peace in every area of my life, in Christ's Name! Amen.

Dear God...

DAY 30
YOU WILL WIN!

> Every Scripture is God-breathed… so that the man of God may be complete and proficient, well-fitted and thoroughly equipped for every good work.
> (2 Timothy 3:16-17)

You can succeed. You can overcome any obstacle through Christ. God has equipped you with everything you need to fulfil your destiny through His Word. That means you are able to do what He has called you to do. You can accomplish your goals. You can fulfil your dreams! You've been armed with strength for every battle.

God is working on your behalf. He has already gone ahead of you and lined up the right situations and the right opportunities. You have everything you need to live the miraculous, victorious life God created you to live!

Today, if you'll stay in faith, it's just a matter of time; victory is on its way. Don't settle where you are. Don't have a weak, defeated mentality. Have the attitude, "I am anointed. I can accomplish my dreams. I can overcome any obstacle. I am empowered by the Creator, and I am thoroughly equipped for every good work that God has called me to do"!

- A PRAYER OF FAITH -

Yahweh, thank You for equipping me for success. Father, I thank You for empowering me by faith. I know that through You I can overcome every obstacle. Help me to stay focused on Your Word and Your plan for my life. God, please help me to walk in Your anointing so that I can do all You've called me to do. I bless You today, in Christ's Name! Amen.

Dear God...

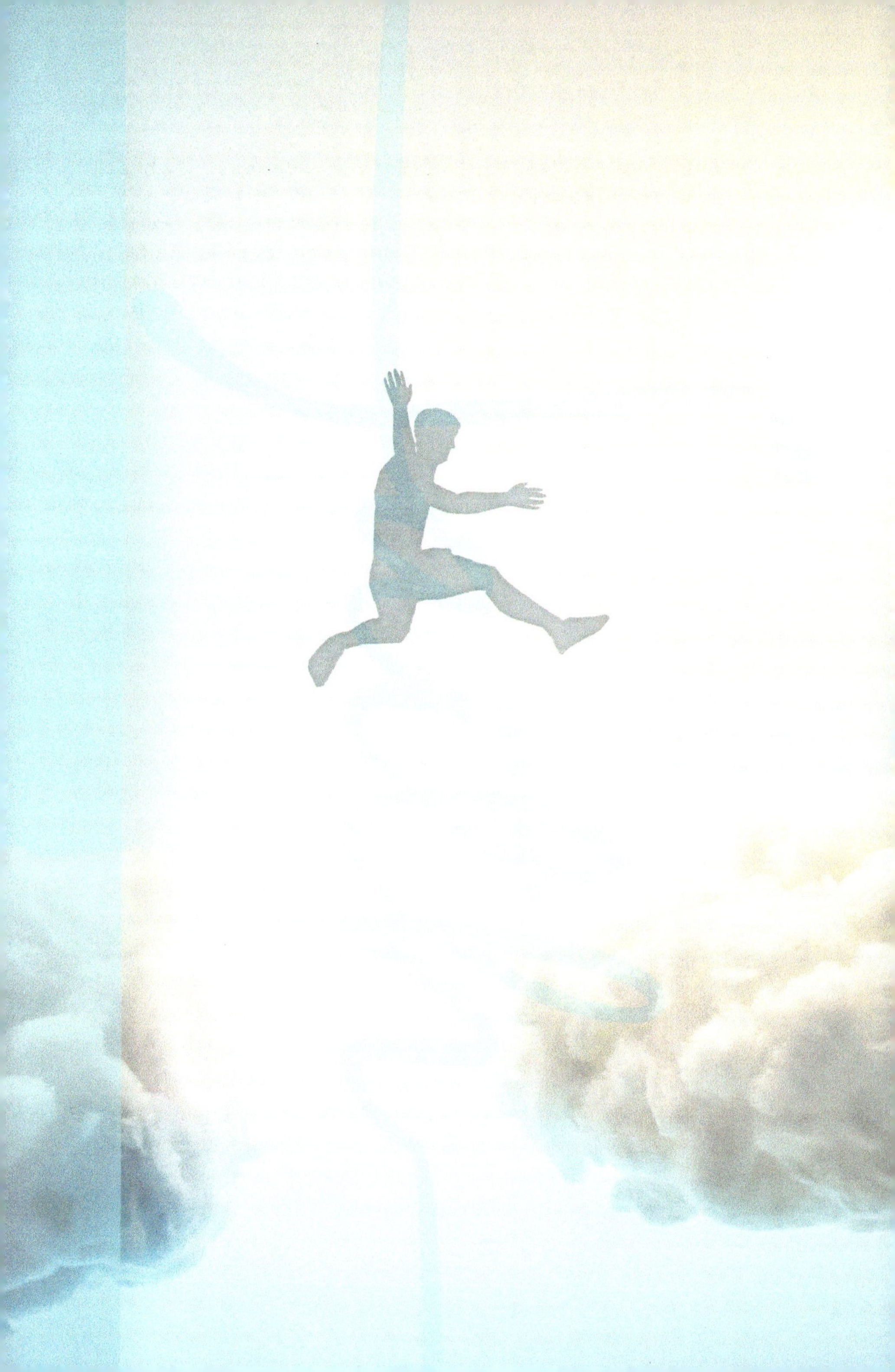

DAILY FAITH HABITS

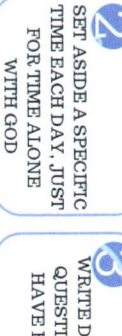

1. CREATE A POEM, SONG, PICTURE ABOUT FAITH

2. SET ASIDE A SPECIFIC TIME EACH DAY, JUST FOR TIME ALONE WITH GOD

3. WRITE DOWN ANY QUESTIONS YOU HAVE FOR GOD

4. PRAY FOR PEACE AND ACCEPTANCE OVER CLOSED DOORS

5. WRITE OUT YOUR DREAMS AND REMIND YOURSELF THEY ARE POSSIBLE

6. HIGHLIGHT YOUR FAVOURITE PROMISES IN THE BIBLE

7. REFLECT OVER YOUR LIFE AND CELEBRATE HOW FAR YOU'VE COME

8. TRY SOMETHING NEW

9. WRITE THE GOOD QUALITIES OF A LOVED ONE WHO HAS PASSED AWAY

10. PRAY THE IMPOSSIBLE PRAYER

11. TREAT YOURSELF TO SOMETHING OR SOMEWHERE THAT MAKES YOU HAPPY

12. WHEN AN INCONVENIENCE COMES, CHOOSE TO SMILE

13. CREATE A PLAYLIST OF SERMONS THAT ENCOURAGE YOU

14. CREATE A PLAYLIST OF GOSPEL SONGS

15. PUT YOUR TOP 10 PROMISES ON A WALL

16. TAKE TIME TO RELEASE ALL THE EMOTIONS YOU'VE BEEN HOLDING ON TO, OVER TO GOD

17. DON'T GIVE UP

18. MAKE A SACRED SPACE FOR PRAYER, AT HOME OR WORK

19. WRITE YOUR WORRIES ON A PIECE OF PAPER, PRAY AND THROW IT AWAY

20. SACRIFICE THE THING THAT IS TAKING YOUR FOCUS FROM GOD

21. PICK FRIENDS WHO ARE POSITIVE, AND GOD-FEARING

22. GET EXCITED ABOUT THE UNKNOWNS OF LIFE – LEAVE IT WITH GOD

23. THANK GOD FOR HIS PROTECTION IN SITUATIONS KNOWN AND UNKNOWN

24. START THAT TASK YOU HAVE BEEN AVOIDING

25. GO TO GOD BEFORE YOUR FRIEND, SOCIAL MEDIA OR YOURSELF

26. CUT OFF ANYTHING YOU WATCH, HEAR OR DO THAT MAKES YOU NEGATIVE

27. COME TO PEACE WITH THE UNREALISTIC BECOMING REALISTIC IN ADVANCE

28. SHARE WITH SOMEBODY YOUR TESTIMONY

29. ASK GOD FOR FORGIVENESS

30. CLAIM THE BLESSINGS OF FAITH

Notes . . .

Notes . . .

Notes...

Notes...

Notes...

TRANSFORM YOUR *Faith*

If you are hurting in this season, remember these points:
He knows. He sees. He understands.
Pain is real - He felt it.
Heartbreak is inevitable - He experienced it. Tears come - His did.
Betrayal happens - Life happens.

Christ is the hope for the broken-hearted. He loves deeply, in ways we can't even fathom. When your heart breaks, when the pain comes, when the whole thing seems like more than you can bear, you can look to God.

The pain won't leave. But His hope will swaddle you tight. His gentle mercy will hold you until you can breathe again. What you long for may never be, but remember He is and is to come.
You can trust that, even in today's hurt.

Be patient and kind to yourself.
Give yourself extra time and space to process your hurt and reach out to others around you if you need extra support.

You may be overwhelmed, bruised, and broken, but there is still goodness to be welcomed and blessings to be claimed this season.

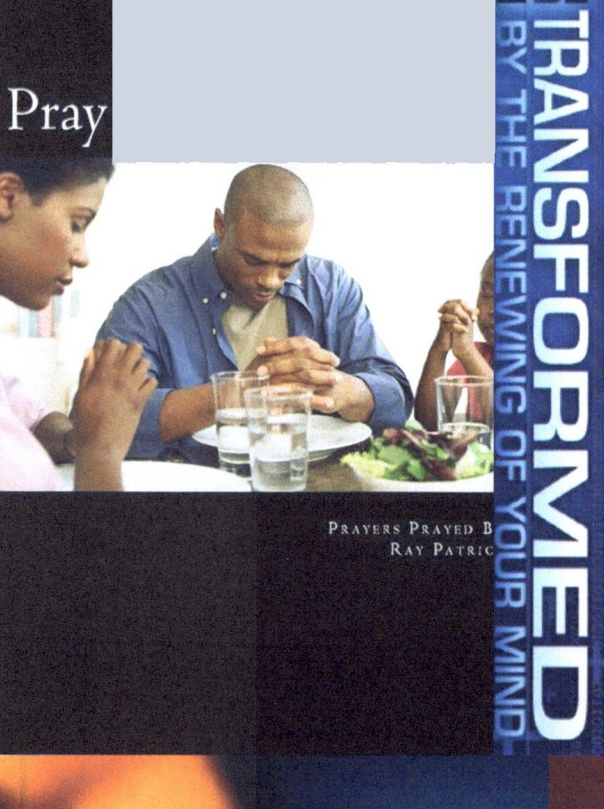

Pray

PRAYERS PRAYED BY
RAY PATRIC

TRANSFORMED
BY THE RENEWING OF YOUR MIND

Transform Your Mind
In 30 Days

Ray A Patric

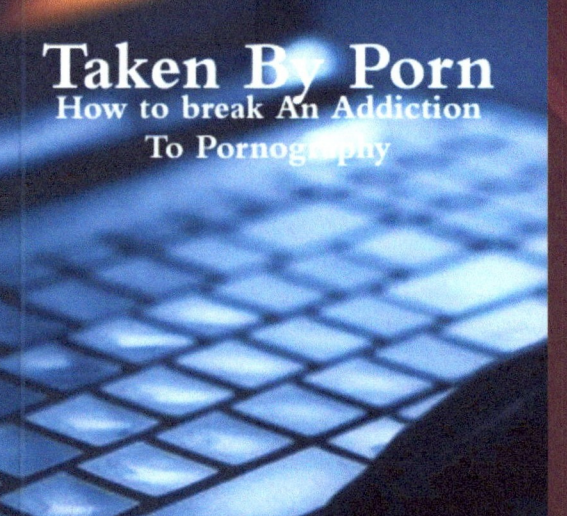

Taken By Porn
How to break An Addiction To Pornography

Ray A Patrick

WARZONE
The Battle For The mind

HOW TO WIN THE BATTLE OF THE MIND

Ray A Patrick